BLACK BOOK OF RIGHTS

In Furtherance of the Civil Rights Movement

Authored by Cedric Martin Hopkins, Esq.
Designed by Isaiah Hopkins

Dedicated to:

Albert Parks and Eliza Parks (pictured)

Albert was born January 31, 1829 and died February 11, 1917. Eliza was born June 25, 1835 and died May 3, 1915. They lived on a plantation in Wilkesboro, North Carolina.

Albert and Eliza were my grandmother's grandparents.

The information contained in this book does not, and is not intended to, constitute specific legal advice. The information may not contain up-to-date legal information. Please consult with a local attorney for any particular legal matter. No reader should act or refrain from acting on the basis of information in this book without first seeking legal advice from local counsel. Only your individual attorney can provide assurances that the information contained herein – and your interpretation of it – is applicable or appropriate to your particular situation.

"One person plus one typewriter constitutes a movement."

       – Pauli Murray

CONTENTS

History of Law Enforcement & Incarceration
8

Police Officers' Attack on Black Americans
12

Prosecutors' and Judges' Attack on
Black Americans
15

Dred Scott v. Sandford
30

Plessy v. Ferguson
34

Brown v. Board of Education of Topeka
39

Evolution of Criminal Investigations
43

Civil Rights Movement
51

The Criminal Justice Regime
56

Your Rights and How to Use Them
58

Terry Stop
61

Miranda Rights
73

Interrogation Tactics
79

Pretextual Traffic Stops
86

Vehicle Searches
89

Search Incident to Arrest
95

Police Knock on Your Door
97

Border Stops
101

DUI Stops
105

Quick Reference Guide
109

Stop and Identify States
120

"Ignorance of each other is what has made unity impossible in the past. Therefore, we need enlightenment. We need more light about each other. Light creates understanding, understanding creates love, love creates patience, and patience creates unity. Once we have more knowledge (light) about each other, we will stop condemning each other and a United front will be brought about." – el-Hajj Malik el-Shabazz

Do you know someone who
would benefit from this book?

Scan this QR code
to order a copy.

This book has a singular goal: to reduce the number of Black men in prison.

To achieve that goal, I will provide you with easy-to-understand explanations of your rights with respect to criminal law and criminal procedure issues, such as when you are interacting with the police. I also hope to educate all people, but especially Black men, about the criminal justice system, which I refer to as the Criminal Justice Regime (more on that later), how it works and how best to either avoid it or position yourself to successfully navigate through the Regime.

My intention is not to make a book that gets used by those individuals who like to provoke the police once they learn their rights. There's no benefit to the advancement of the goal of reducing Black men in prison by provoking the police on the street.

Learning your rights with respect to interacting with the police is a responsibility that is a carryover from, and a continuation of, the Civil Rights Movement. Previously, you didn't have those civil rights by law, now you don't have them by practice. By learning your rights and practicing those rights in a responsible manner, you are joining and continuing the Civil Rights Movement.

It is your responsibility to learn those rights and then exercise them in a manner that counterattacks how the Criminal Justice Regime is relentlessly and systematically attacking you.

This book holds you accountable for learning your rights and then exercising those rights in a responsible way that if you enter that Regime, you will provide your lawyer with a sword to defend you with. Do not wield the sword that these rights provide by yourself; a lawyer will do that on your behalf. By learning these rights you become the shield in the battle against the Regime.

A person who knows their rights and exercises those rights can still have their rights violated by the police. Just because you inform an officer of your rights doesn't mean they will, 1) know your rights, or 2) respect those rights. In those cases, you should not physically fight back against the officer. **Ever.**

But, by knowing your rights and expressing those rights to the officer, even if you are being arrested, you will improve your chances against any charges that get filed against you and you will arm your attorney with the artillery they need to properly fight your case. You will also have the evidence you need with respect to any litigation that may arise between you and the police department based on any police misconduct.

Remember, *you* are now the continuation of the Civil Rights Movement. We are living in a peculiar stage of the Civil Rights Movement. I often hear people speak of the Civil Rights Movement as something that happened in the past. If you Google, "Civil Rights Movement," it will display an end date, as though the movement is over. Some argue that we no longer have Black leaders to lead us in the fights that we are fighting today. But the Black leaders of the past did their job;

they got laws passed that provide you with equal rights.

Now, the position of leadership must shift from a few leaders like we had in the past, to each of us serving as a leader in the Movement. The fight now is to take the rights that the previous leaders obtained for us, learn them, and then exercise them diligently and responsibly.

As I view the things going on today in America, I see that the fights that were fought decades ago to get legislation passed was only the groundwork for the fight that needs to continue. That's why the Civil Rights Movement is still upon us, and that's why we are each now the Malcolm's, Thurgood's, Pauli Murray's, Baldwin's, Charles Houston's, Jackie's, Medgar's and Martin's.

In the past, we looked to trailblazers to lead the Movement. Black Americans were made to feel, and felt, inferior to "white"[1]

---

[1] I wrote "white" in quotation marks because white should not be used to describe individuals the same way Black is used. While every white person may not know their true ancestry or heritage, they have not had those lines fragmented like Black people did during slavery – "white" people are better able to trace their roots to a specific country. Black people's ancestors were taken from a country and records were not kept of where those people were taken from, only to whom they were sold. Their last name became the last name of their slave master and missus. As such, the generic, "Black," is used as a catchall, whereas the divisive "white" is not needed.

The term "white" saw its origins following Bacon's Rebellion in the Virginia colony. In 1676, Nathaniel Bacon, Jr. and his supporters (made up of Black and white indentured servants and African slaves) revolted against Virginia Governor William Berkeley and wealthy tobacco plantation owners. Poor, white people in Europe were promised 50 acres of land in America if they would travel to America and work for a plantation

Americans so it took a courageous few to stand up to an unjust government and oppressive practices. Those trailblazers worked diligently to make things appear equal on paper. Today, we are the continuation of the Movement, and the Movement is

---

owner for 3 to 7 years. The plantation owners were given those 50 acres for every person who came to work on their plantation. As the indentured servants began to fulfill the terms of the indenture, the land they were promised became scarce. Bacon and his followers felt the land should be taken from the Native Americans in the West but Governor Berkeley resisted such an approach. The rebellion then occurred.

Following the rebellion, Virginia enacted the Virginia Slave Codes of 1705, which controlled the interactions between poor, white people and free Black people and African slaves. The laws were used to control the sharp rise in Black population due to slavery, and to keep white colonist separate from Black people so as to avoid those two groups uniting again against the government. As such, the "white" and "Black" distinctions were formed.

happening each day, with every interaction you have with someone, with the way you carry yourself, and with the way you invoke your rights.

So this book is my attempt at an answer to the question, "What happens next?" It's clear there is a systemic problem with policing in America, especially when it comes to Black Americans, particularly Black men. As you will see in the next few pages, light has been shed on the problematic policing practicing in America for over a century. Shining light on the problem has done little to nothing to stop the problem. So, again, me arming you with your rights and explaining how to use those rights will put you in a better position to not become another Black man in a jail cell. The pioneers fought for those rights, now it's your time to learn and exercise them.

History of Law Enforcement & Incarceration

If you're paying attention then you know the United States of America is in the business of incarcerating individuals for profit. The United States houses 25% of the world's prisoners while making up only 5% of the world population. The flagship product for that business is Black Americans.

Within the United States, Black men account for 40.2% of the total prison population while accounting for only 6.5% of the country's population. As a result, 1 in 3 Black Americans is likely to be incarcerated during their lifetime, compared to 1 in 17 for their white counterpart.

No one is coming to save Black Americans, particularly Black men, from being targeted at such a disproportionate rate. And make no mistake, you are being targeted.

John Ehrlichman, President Richard Nixon's Attorney and Assistant to the President for Domestic Affairs, was on record explaining the United States' planned attack on Black Americans during Nixon's presidency: "The Nixon campaign in 1968 and the Nixon White House after that, had two enemies: the antiwar left and Black people. You understand what I'm saying? We knew we couldn't make it illegal to be either against the war or Black, but by getting the public to associate the hippies with marijuana and Blacks with heroin, and **then criminalizing both heavily, we could disrupt those communities.** We could arrest their leaders, raid their homes, break up their meetings, and **vilify them night after night on the evening news.** Did we know we were lying about the drugs? Of course we did."

In 1981, Lee Atwater, Ronald Reagan's Campaign Strategist, was secretly taped explaining how Ronald Regan and the United States government continued the terror and attack on Black Americans: "...In other words you start out in 1954 by saying, 'nigger, nigger,

nigger. By 1968 you can't say nigger; that hurts you. It backfires. So you say stuff like forced-bussing, state's rights and all that stuff. You're getting so abstract now; you're talking about cutting taxes ... and all of these things you're talking about are totally economic things, **and the byproduct of them is Blacks get hurt worse than whites.**"

Ronald Regan ramped up Nixon's War on Drugs in the 1980s, including creating disproportionate mandatory minimum sentencing schemes for crack cocaine compared to powder cocaine. To receive the prison sentence that was required for one ounce of crack cocaine a person would have to possess almost 3 kilos of powder cocaine.

Newt Gingrich, Former Speaker of the House of Representatives, recounted, "We absolutely should have treated crack and [powder] cocaine as exactly the same thing. **I think it was an enormous burden on the Black community** but it also fundamentally violated a sense of core fairness."

These are just a few, undeniable statements that unequivocally prove that the United States government has continued to target Black Americans since the Civil Rights Movement. Obviously, prior to the Civil Rights Movement, the targeting was evident and accepted, just as Lee Atwater described. The targeting is still practiced; it's just more abstract.

In the 1970's, the prison population was approximately 350,000 inmates. Today, that number has skyrocketed to over 2.3 million. The targeting that Ehrlichman, Atwater, Nixon, Regan, Hoover, Bill Clinton and others engaged in towards Black Americans made that number climb as fast as it did.

Some would say, well if Black people weren't committing crimes, then they wouldn't go to prison. You are overlooking, either intentionally or neglectfully, the entire three-tiered Criminal Justice Regime that has been deployed against Black Americans. Those three tiers are 1) the police, 2) prosecutors, and 3) judges.

<u>Police Officers' Attack on Black Americans</u>

A team of researchers conducted a seven-year study[2] (published in May, 2020) that analyzed approximately 95 million traffic stops by 56 police agencies. The data from the study mirrors the statements and practices that were explained by Atwater and Ehrlichman: Black people are being unjustly targeted by police officers.

The study confirmed the "Driving While Black" experience of many Black Americans.

The data revealed, of course, that Black Americans were much more likely to be pulled over than whites. This is the known bias and racist practices that occur. The data that cements the "Driving While Black" bias that exists is the fact that the disparity at which Black drivers are pulled over lessens at night, when police are less able to distinguish

---

[2] Pierson, E., Simoiu, C., Overgoor, J. et al. A large-scale analysis of racial disparities in police stops across the United States. Nat Hum Behav 4, 736–745 (2020). https://doi.org/10.1038/s41562-020-0858-1

the race of the driver. When the police officers could not determine the race of a driver, Black Americans and white people were pulled over at normal rates. The study also found that Black Americans were more likely to be searched after a stop, though **whites were more likely to be found with illicit drugs.**

Another study from 2019[3] examined police stops in Cincinnati, Ohio. This study also found that Black motorists were 30 percent more likely to be pulled over than white motorists. Again, police have created the crime of "Driving While Black." Black motorists also comprised 76% of arrests following a traffic stop despite making up 43% of the city's population. This study, like many others, showed through the data that **searches of white motorists are more likely**

---

[3]https://www.cincinnati.com/story/opinion/2019/12/20/editorial-racial-disparities-police-stops-demands-attention/2666685001/

to turn up contraband than searches of Black motorists.

The California Racial and Identity Profiling Advisory Board[4] analyzed and reported on approximately 1.8 million police stops by the eight largest law enforcement agencies in California. As suspected, the Board found that Black motorists were stopped at a rate 2.5 times higher than the per capita rate of white motorists. The report also found that Black motorists were far more likely to be stopped for "reasonable suspicion" (as opposed to actually breaking a law) and were three times more likely than any other group to be searched, **even though searches of white drivers were more likely to turn up contraband.**

---

[4] https://www.usnews.com/news/best-states/california/articles/2020-01-02/report-california-cops-more-likely-to-stop-black-drivers

Study after study continues to highlight the racist and biased practices of police departments all across the United States. As noted earlier, the police are relentlessly attacking Black men with the goal of incarcerating as many as possible. But the racist police practices are only the start. Once the police arrest you, you then are facing another equally racist and biased judicial system that begins with the prosecutors and ends with the judges.

Prosecutors' and Judges' Assault on Black Americans

The studies examining prosecutors' decision-making and judges' practices in the Criminal Justice Regime have similar findings as those studies observing police behavior towards Black Americans.

A 2013 study found that after adjusting for numerous other variables, federal prosecutors were almost twice as likely to bring charges carrying mandatory minimum prison sentences against Black defendants as against white defendants accused of similar crimes.

A 2016 review[5] of nearly 474,000 criminal cases in Hampton Roads, Virginia, found that white defendants were more likely to receive a favorable plea agreement that resulted in no jail time for drug offenses. While facing charges of drug distribution, 48% of white defendants received plea bargains with no jail time, as compared to 22% of Black defendants. Among those with prior criminal records who pleaded guilty to robbery, 36% of white defendants received no jail time, compared to 8% of Black defendants.

A 2017 study of about 48,000 criminal cases in Wisconsin showed that white defendants were 25% more likely than Black defendants to have prosecutors offer plea agreements that would result in their most serious charge being dismissed. Among defendants facing misdemeanor charges that could carry a

---

[5] https://www.dailypress.com/news/dp-nws-sunshine-disparities-20160317-story.html

sentence of incarceration, white defendants were 75% more likely to have those charges dropped, dismissed or reduced to a charge that did not include such a punishment.

A 2019 review of academic literature by the Prison Policy Initiative[6] found that "in large urban areas, Black felony defendants are over 25% more likely than white defendants to be held pretrial" when charged with similar crimes. Nationally, the review found that young Black men were about 50% more likely to be detained during pretrial proceedings than white defendants, and on average were given bail amounts that were twice as high.

Even before Black Americans have interaction with the police, they are subject to attacks by educators. Data released in 2016 from the Department of Education[7] found

[6]https://www.prisonpolicy.org/blog/2019/10/09/pre trial_race/

[7]https://www.usatoday.com/story/news/2016/06/07/black-students-nearly-4x-likely-suspended/85526458/

that Black students were nearly four times more likely to be suspended than white students.

The studies you just read about pertain to the Criminal Justice Regime but these are numerous studies that pinpoint the exact same targeting that is done towards Black Americans in just about every area of life, including the foster care system, employment opportunities, housing, and many others.

At this point, if anyone denies that the United States, in almost every facet of life, is attacking Black Americans then they are doing so purposefully and irresponsibility.

The three-tiered Criminal Justice Regime is what produces the disproportionate number of Black American criminals, not Black Americans committing more crimes than whites. Remember, in just about all of the studies examining vehicle stops, the white motorists were more likely to have contraband in their vehicle.

And the racially disparate outcomes that the studies show are occurring regardless of the race of the police, prosecutors or judges; it's the Regime (and all other systems and institutions) that produces these results. And it does so because the United States has yet to make the transformation of viewing Black people as equivalent human beings.

The studies that underscore the concept that Black people are still not viewed as equivalent human beings are the studies that show how Black Americans are systemically undertreated for pain relative to white Americans in the medical field.

For example, a study[8] done in 2016 revealed that nearly half of first and second year

---

[8] Hoffman, K. M., Trawalter, S., Axt, J. R., & Oliver, M. N. (2016). Racial bias in pain assessment and treatment recommendations, and false beliefs about biological differences between blacks and whites. *Proceedings of the National Academy of Sciences of the United States of America*, *113*(16), 4296–4301. https://doi.org/10.1073/pnas.1516047113

medical students (along with white laypeople) believed that Black people have thicker skin than white people, and perceived Black people as experiencing less pain than white people. These medical students made less accurate medical treatment recommendations for Black people than for white people.

There are dozens, if not hundreds, of similar studies that prove the continued dehumanization of Black Americans.[9]

What the studies show is that "white" America is still dealing from the bottom of the deck – a deck they stacked against Black Americans – when it comes to race in America. And when Black Americans show the hand they are dealt, white America accuses them of "playing the race card." White America created the deck of cards and has been in complete control of dealing out the cards as it sees fit.

---

[9] https://www.ncbi.nlm.nih.gov/pmc/articles/PMC4843483/citedby/

Black America has endured through slavery, watched the 13th Amendment get passed to "end" slavery, suffered through the Jim Crow era, overturned Plessy v. Ferguson, fought to get the Voting Rights, Civil Rights and Fair Housing Acts passed, and now, as you may hear from time to time, Black people have the same rights as everyone else. Apparently, because the historic events described above happened, some people say Black people are on a level playing field, along with everyone else in the United States.

They ignore the long lasting, demeaning, demoralizing effects of the Jim Crow Era. As you will see, the Supreme Court based their decision in Brown v. Board of Education on the social science of what the Jim Crow laws did to the mentality of Black Americans – irreversible damage. Has that damage been reversed in less than half of the amount of the time it took to dispense it?

Habitually, it takes longer to heal from a wound than it took to get injured, whether that's physical or mental. Jim Crow was

around, legally, for approximately 70 years.
We have been living without the Jim Crow
laws for about 55 years (Jim Crow practices
are still occurring, however).

Jim Crow prevented my dad from visiting
Santa Claus at the local department store
because the entrance for Black Americans was
around the corner from the main entrance
and led to a basement where Jim Crow and
white Americans told him he could shop. His
birthday is December 24, 1939, and Jim Crow
laws "ended" around 1960, so he never saw
Santa as a child in the store like you did.

But some still think slavery and Jim Crow
ended so long ago.

Legal, wholesale slavery ended in December
of 1895 with the passage of the 13th
Amendment. Jim Crow laws were overturned
in the 1950's, and the Civil Rights Act was
passed in 1964. Those events didn't stop
racism or its effects. The idea of racism and
oppression, or the effects of those, being

extinguished by the passing of laws is nonsensical.

Slavery, and its rippling effects, is like a virus. It didn't just go away because a law was passed. The slave mind still exists in both white and Black Americans. A large number of Black and white people still feel how the U.S. Supreme Court Chief Justice did in the Dred Scott case when he reasoned that Black people are inferior to white people; that mindset is a carryover from slavery. That feeling and conviction are displayed throughout society, in a number of ways.

One way that feeling is exhibited is the way in which law enforcement in the United States targets Black Americans.

The truth of the matter is that Black Americans are not on a level playing field when it comes to almost all aspects of daily life. But because certain events have happened (slavery ending, Jim Crow era over, successful Civil Rights campaign), and people can point to those events, they say the playing field is now level. Those people will argue that "the past is the past, and things are different now, everyone has the same opportunities."

But, "facts are a stubborn thing." – John Adams.

The facts show and the studies prove that Black Americans are disproportionately pulled over by police, searched by police and arrested by police. That harassment has an effect on a Black man who is driving to a job interview that white Americans don't have to address or grapple with in their lives.

The facts show that prosecutors seek charges (and more severe charges) disproportionately against Black Americans than any other group.

The facts show that judges choose to hand out disproportionately harsher prison sentences to Black defendants than any other racial group of defendants.

Again, we are not on a level playing field.

The closest thing that represents the playing field Black Americans are playing on are the studies examining the rates at which Black Americans are pulled over in their vehicles. As previously discussed, a number of these studies examine the pull over rates during the day compared to pull over rates during the night. During the day, police are significantly more likely to pull over a Black driver compared to a white driver. **But during the night, when the police are no longer able to racially profile Black drivers, police pull over Black and white drivers at the same rate.**

Now pay close attention to this: In several of those studies it has been proven that when police conduct searches of those vehicles, there is a much higher likelihood that illegal contraband will be found in the vehicles driven by white drivers than Black drivers. Nevertheless, police officers continue to target Black drivers at a disproportionate rate, and a subset of society believes Black people commit more crimes.

Black Americans are not on a level playing field with their white counterparts.

The Voting Rights Act of 1965 assured there would be no more racial discrimination in voting. But the Black vote remains under attack.

The Civil Rights Act of 1968 was legislation that outlawed discrimination and banned racial segregation in schools, in the workplace and in public facilities. At the risk of stating the obvious, discrimination remains prevalent in all of those places.

The Fair Housing Act of 1968 was supposed to end discrimination when it came to finding a home. Illegal discriminating housing practices are used against Black Americans today.

Never in the U.S. Constitution is the word "slave" written. But the document made sure to govern slavery.

The 13th Amendment promised to free slaves, but the drafters of that Amendment made sure to keep slavery.

The 13th Amendment was written into the U.S. Constitution to address the Privileges and Immunities Clause. The Privileges and Immunities Clause sounds harmless enough: "the citizens of each state shall be entitled to all privileges and immunities of citizens in the several states." This means, essentially, that one state cannot treat its residents any differently than out-of-state residents. That's Clause 1 of Section 2 of Article 4 of the U.S. Constitution.

Clause 2 of that Section gives states the right to have people brought back to their state if the person commits a crime and flees the state.

The 13th Amendment addresses Clause 3: "No person held to service or labor in one State, under the laws thereof, escaping into another, shall, in consequence of any law or regulation therein, be discharged from such service or labor, but shall be delivered up on claim of the party to whom such service or labor may be due."

Clause 3 was written to serve as the fugitive slave clause. A slave master could go into another state and retrieve their slave if the slave crossed into any other state.

The 13th Amendment was drafted and touted by many to "abolish slavery." It did not do that in either the wording of the Amendment itself, or in practice.

The 13th Amendment reads, "Neither slavery nor involuntary servitude, except as a punishment for crime whereof the party shall have been duly convicted, shall exist within the United States, or any place subject to their jurisdiction."

So if on December 5, 1865 you owned slaves and then, on December 6, 1865, those slaves were freed, based on the words of the 13th Amendment, all you had to do was show that the slave committed a crime and then that slave would have to continue to work for you.

The slave industry was a billion dollar industry in the 1800's. The people and institutions that relied on that industry were not going to let that workforce simply disappear. The states did not want to free the slaves and thereby lose their assets. They resisted. It was incumbent upon the survival of America to criminalize the recently freed slaves. In fact, four days after Colin Kaepernick played in the 2013 Super Bowl, Mississippi finally got around to ratifying the 13th Amendment, on February 7, 2013.

Like the slave industry, the prison industry today is a billion dollar business. Black bodies serve as the lifeline that keeps those billions of dollars being made year after year by the government and corporations.

Dred Scott v. Sandford

I believe the law enforcement issue in America starts with the momentous United States Supreme Court case of Dred Scott v. Sandford.[10] In that case, the Court was answering the question: "Can a negro, whose ancestors were imported into this country, and sold as slaves, become a member of the political community formed and brought into existence by the Constitution of the United States, and as such become entitled to all the rights, and privileges, and immunities, guarantied by that instrument to the citizen? One of which rights is the privilege of suing in a court of the United States in the cases specified in the Constitution."

It's answer[11] was as follows: "In the opinion of the court, the legislation and histories of

---

[10] *Dred Scott v. Sandford, 60 U.S. 393 (1957)*

[11] This same Court opined that Native Americans "would be entitled to all the rights and privileges which would belong to an emigrant from any other foreign people."

the times, and the language used in the Declaration of Independence, show, that neither the class of persons who had been imported as slaves, nor their descendants, whether they had become free or not, were then acknowledged as a part of the people, nor intended to be included in the general words used in that memorable instrument."

The Dred Scott Court went on to decide that "[Negros] had for more than a century before been regarded as beings of an inferior order, and altogether unfit to associate with the white race, either in social or political relations; and **so far inferior, that they had no rights which the white man was bound to respect**; and that the negro might justly and lawfully be reduced to slavery for his benefit. He was bought and sold, and treated as an ordinary article of merchandise and traffic, whenever a profit could be made by it."

Ultimately, the Supreme Court ruled that Black people ("Negros"), whether enslaved or free, could not be American citizens and

therefore did not have standing to sue in
federal court.

The Court further declared the Missouri
Compromise of 1820 unconstitutional and
barred Congress from freeing slaves within
federal territories.

The Dred Scott decision cemented in people's
minds (Black and white) that Black people
were not equal with white people. And within
that decision you can begin to unearth why
Black-on-Black crime persists.[12] In its analysis,
the Court looked to laws in the United States
that demonstrated why Black people were
inferior to support its conclusion. One of
those laws was in Massachusetts: "If any

---

[12] A 2016 study found that in Louisiana, killers of
white victims were 14 times more likely to be executed
than killers of black victims. Black men who killed
white women were 30 times more likely to get the
death penalty than black men who killed black men.
Those convicted of killing white people were also less
likely to have their sentences overturned on appeal, and
Louisiana hasn't executed a white person for killing a
black person since 1752.

negro or mulatto shall presume to smite or strike any person of the English or other Christian nation, such negro or mulatto shall be severely whipped, at the discretion of the justices before whom the offender shall be convicted."

No such law existed for violence towards a Black person, presumably because Black people were not thought to be people, only property. That was the thinking of not only white people for hundreds of years – *hundreds of years* – but of Black people too. It was engrained in everyone's way of thinking and acting that Black people's lives did not matter. So it was, and is, no big deal for a Black person to kill another Black person.

Then the Civil War occurred and the 13th Amendment was introduced and ratified in December of 1865. And in 1892, Homer Plessy decided to sit in a "whites only" railway car to challenge a Louisiana law that required separate railway cars for blacks and whites.

Plessy v. Ferguson

The United States Supreme Court, in Plessy v. Ferguson,[13] solidified the end of the Reconstruction era (a series of laws that were enacted following the Civil War to protect the rights of Black Americans, and federal troops who were deployed in order to enforce those laws) by deciding that the Louisiana state law permitting segregation was constitutional and that separate treatment did not imply the inferiority of Black Americans.

Enter Jim Crow.

If Congress was going to take away the institution that legally ensured Black people felt, and were, inferior to white people (that institution being slavery), then the justices of the United States Supreme Court would make sure to implant another institution: Jim Crow laws.

---

[13] *Plessy v. Ferguson, 163 U.S. 537 (1896)*

The Plessy decision created Jim Crow laws. Jim Crow laws were laws that permitted anything and everything in society to be separate (one for Black people and one for white people). There were separate drinking fountains for Black and white people, separate entrances to stores, etc.

The Jim Crow laws were applied to every aspect of life and all aspects of society were segregated – housing, hospitals, phone booths, schools, food, parks, cemeteries, text books, drinking fountains, entrances, everything. There were even separate trees used for the execution of Black and white Americans following conviction of a capital offense. This was Jim Crow.

The Plessy decision gave rise to the phrase, "separate, but equal." And this phrase was used by white Americans to argue the point that Black people are on a level playing field with whites and have every opportunity to succeed like they do. A familiar battle cry as we hear today.

A man named Charles Houston killed Jim Crow.

Charles Houston, an attorney, trained Thurgood Marshall. While doing so, he attacked Jim Crow.

Houston believed that discrimination in the education system was symbolic of all other severe discriminations that were occurring against Black people. The Equal Protection Clause of the 14th Amendment was the foundation Houston used to attack Jim Crow.

The 14th Amendment essentially declares that all United States citizens would enjoy equal protections of the laws. The opening clause, "All persons born or naturalized in the United States and subject to the jurisdiction thereof, are citizens of the United States and of the State wherein they reside," was drafted to combat the justices finding in the Dred Scott that Black people, even if not a slave, are not entitled to citizenship in the United States.

Houston traveled around the United States documenting the inequities in the education system. He showed that teachers' salaries were not uniform, the facilities were not equivalent and the textbooks were not alike.

In 1932-33, South Carolina education expenditures totaled approximately $11.5 million. Of that amount, $10.2M was allocated for whites and $1.3M was allocated for Black Americans. The pay for teachers: $7,108 for white teachers, and $1,246 for Black teachers.

Houston's first case was against the discriminating admission practices of the University of Maryland Law School. Houston proved that a potential law student, Donald Murray, was denied admission based on race. Thurgood Marshall and Houston tried the case. The court ruled for Murray and determined that the university must integrate the law school.

In Gaines v. Missouri, Houston sued on behalf of a student who was denied entrance into a law school (the only law school) in

Missouri. The student, Gaines, was a citizen of Missouri. In a unanimous decision, the lower court ruled that since there were law schools available in other states that would accept Black Americans, Gaines would have to go to one of the schools bordering Missouri. Houston took the case to the United States Supreme Court and the Court ruled that Missouri's position violated the 14th Amendment – that even if state was going to provide separate education, it couldn't provide separate education outside of the state.

Houston[14] continued the fight against Jim Crow by proving inequities in teachers' salaries, transportation, public accommodations, housing and labor, and continued to provide additional precedents for the final assault on Plessy and Jim Crow: Brown v. Board of Education.

---

[14] Charles Hamilton Houston died of heart failure on April 22, 1950, at the age of 54, four years before Brown v. Board of Education was decided.

As Charles Houston once told Thurgood Marshall, "There's no law on our side? Let's make some."

Brown v. Board of Education of Topeka

On May 17, 1954, the United States Supreme Court decided Brown v. Board of Education.[15] Grounding its decision in social science rather than legal precedent, the Supreme Court, in a unanimous decision, decided that to separate children based solely on race **generates feeling of inferiority that affects Black children's hearts and minds in a way unlikely to be undone.** The Court reasoned that Jim Crow laws in education instilled a sense of inferiority that had a hugely detrimental effect on the education and personal growth of African American children.

Plessy is overruled; Jim Crow is dead, but not really.

---

[15] *Brown v. Board of Education of Topeka, 347 U.S. 483 (1954)*

Following the Brown decision, there was predictable, yet overwhelming "white backlash," and Southern states defiantly retained segregation practices and laws and violently rejected Black Americans using the same facilities they used. They demanded that Black Americans continue to use the inferior facilities.

Following the Brown decision, Autherine Lucy, a young Black woman, believed that her dream of earning a degree in library science could actually occur. She proudly enrolled (after obtaining a court order to do so) at the all-white University of Alabama on February 3, 1956. While the court had granted her the right to attend the university, the white citizens of Alabama did everything in their power to prevent Autherine from getting an education. Students, adults and even groups from outside of Alabama shouted racial epithets, threw eggs, sticks and rocks at Autherine, and even started riots over her enrollment. As a result of this white backlash, the University voted to expelled her on

February 6, 1956, "in order to ensure her personal safety."

The Board of Regents didn't overturn Ms. Lucy's expulsion until 1988. She immediately enrolled back into the University the following year and graduated in 1992 with a master's degree in elementary education. Her daughter, Grazia, also enrolled into the University as an undergraduate at the same time.

What happened to Autherine when she tried to get an education at a university that was not deemed inferior occurred to thousands of other Black Americans, stories told and untold.

All throughout the United States, in response to Brown v. Board of Education, white Americans in cities and towns created private schools to keep white students from having to mix with Black students. From 1950 to 1965 private school enrollment grew at unprecedented rates all over the nation, with the South having the largest growth.

This vehement resistance to Black Americans being included in, and protected by the U.S. Constitution was evident in the newly formed "heritage" Southern whites displayed by flying the confederate flag.[16] The vast majority of those flags were first raised in the 1960's, during the Civil Rights Movement, nearly 100 years after the Civil War ended. Of course, following the Civil War, and for almost 100 years thereafter, the confederate flag was nowhere to be seen. It wasn't until Black Americans began to *appear* equal to white Americans did that flag make its appearance.

This same reaction was shown in recent times when Black Americans declared that they mattered. In response, many white Americans responded that all people mattered and began to fly a new version of the American flag that

---

[16] The Confederate States of America used three different flags from 1861 to 1865, none of which were the contemporary confederate flag used by racists today. The confederate flag, otherwise known as the "Dixie swastika," used by racists today is the battle flag of the Army of Northern Virginia and Army of Tennessee.

included a blue, red and/or green stripe. More and more of these Americans who oppose the position that Black lives matter are beginning to hoist all-black American flags to show their opposition to Black people fighting against the evidence shown in the studies cited above and getting closer to achieving equality. These are the same people who would have, and perhaps did, hoist the confederate flag in the 1960's when Black Americans were fighting for equality and the right to have the U.S. Constitution apply to them fairly.

Evolution of Criminal Investigations

Up until approximately 1850, judges would primarily conduct criminal investigations. During pretrial proceedings, judges would question witnesses and the defendants in order to ascertain the facts of the case. The judges performed these investigations from the bench.

Starting around 1850,[17] investigation responsibilities moved from judges to newly formed, large-scale police departments. Those police departments were largely corrupt and engaged in terrorizing both white and Black populations. Within the white population, poor white immigrants (Polish, Irish, etc.) were the ones being terrorized. In other words, the police officers would focus their attention on both, the poor citizens as well as the Black citizens.

The police departments and police officers in the North mirrored the law enforcement practices of the Slave Patrols in the South. Slave Patrols were used to control slaves in the South and to prevent or catch runaway slaves. The men who made up the patrols were known to use brutal tactics against slaves.

---

[17] Police departments in the United States were modeled off of police departments formed in England in 1829 after the Parliament passed the Metropolitan Police Act, which created the first organized police force in England.

Police departments in the North used the same brutal tactics against the poor and Black people in the North that the Slave Patrols did against Black people in the South. These tactics were largely against poor, white immigrants because Black people made up a very small percentage of the population in the North.

At the turn of the century, starting around 1910, the Great Migration took place where a large number of Black Americans fled from the South and headed to northern cities.

The police then shifted their focus of terror from poor, white immigrants to the new Black population. In fact, the white immigrants who were once terrorized switched from being Irish or Polish and just became "white." This was done because while the white population made distinguished groups within itself prior to the arrival of Black people, they had to establish a new pecking order, of which Black people were on the bottom and white people were on top, similar to what occurred following Bacon's Rebellion.

The hostility and intimidation that was once shown towards the Irish was now directed towards the Black population. And now, with the arrival of the Black population, the Irish simply became "white" and the police would "protect" the Irish in any confrontation with Black citizens, which is what started the first "race riots" in the United States.

An examination of any race riot in the United States shows a precipitating event of either police brutality or, in the earliest riots, police failing to protect Black citizens from getting attacked by white citizens.

When Black Americans moved to the North they looked for housing and jobs. The jobs they were allowed to accept were the jobs that the Irish previously worked. And the housing that Black Americans were permitted to occupy were among the Irish and other "lowly" white immigrants. This clashing of the two groups created hostility between the Irish and Black populations.

The Irish citizens used intimidation tactics and violence to deter Black Americans from the housing and jobs the Irish desired. The police refused to answer the Black Americans' call for help or actually attacked the Black Americans in response. Black Americans had no protection. Riots then occurred.

As an illustration, in one particular disturbing but far too normal case, a young boy, 17-year-old Eugene Williams, was swimming in Lake Michigan and swam into the "white section" of the lake. The white people on the beach, 29th Street Beach, killed him by stoning him to death. A police officer was present and Black Americans asked him to protect the boy. The police officer did nothing. The Black population became outraged and demanded justice. Because the Black population became outraged and had the audacity to demand justice, the white community attacked the Black community.

On July 27, 1919, the Chicago riots began when white citizens advanced into Black neighborhoods. "Many white Chicagoans felt

African Americans had been getting out of their place. So they used this opportunity to remind them of their place in a subordinate and second-class position. All of those things sort of came to a head at that moment," said Julius Jones, Assistant Curator with the Chicago History Museum. The police joined the white Chicagoans in the seven-day riot and a total of 23 Black people were killed (15 white people were killed). The vast majority of people arrested were Black Americans.

Several different researchers during this time came to the same conclusion: racism and police brutality was routine in almost every police department around the country that was studied.

In response to the overwhelming police brutality and corruption that was occurring, in 1931, President Herbert Hoover commissioned then Attorney General, George Wickersham to do extensive reporting on law enforcement in the United States. This created the National Commission on Law Observance and Enforcement, unofficially referred to as the Wickersham Commission.

One section of the final report from Wickersham is called the Report on Lawlessness in Law Enforcement (the Report), and has been quoted by many courts and used to describe the type of interrogation a suspect would likely endure in most police stations up to and through the 1930s.

The first section of the Report, "The Third Degree," explains the conditions and treatment that suspects faced during an interrogation with the police. The Report explains that the third degree means "the employment of methods which inflict suffering, physical or mental, upon a person in order to obtain information about a crime." Those methods included threats with weapons, beating with fists, constant awakening at night, deprivation of food, beatings with a rubber hose, use of blinding lights during questioning, prolonged questioning, and other severe tactics were reported to be in use throughout the country.

Following the Wickersham Commission, which failed to specifically address police brutality against Black Americans and only focused on issues relating to white citizens, police departments began having standards for hiring police departments and hired only white police officers. This led to the legitimizing of police targeting Black citizens disproportionately. This raised the crime statistics, disproportionately, for Black crime. The police, therefore, felt justified in overpolicing Black citizens.

Police were able to target Black citizens in the horrific manner in which they did because the laws permitted them to do so. The Jim Crow laws and how those laws were implemented in the United States engrained in white and Black people that Black people were inferior.

During the 1930s, 1940s and 1950s, Black Americans felt the United States should allow them to exercise their newly provided rights of being equal under the law and to live without facing discrimination. Martin Luther King, Jr. summed up this feeling the day before he was killed during his "I've Been to the Mountaintop" speech when he said, "All we say to America is, 'Be true to what you said on paper.'"

Civil Rights Movement

What is commonly known as the Civil Rights Movement started following the 1954 Brown decision. In 1956, the Montgomery, Alabama buses were integrated. In 1957, the schools in Little Rock, Arkansas were integrated. And there were numerous marches and sit-ins in the 1960's, and the voices of many Black leaders were birthed during this time and the Voting Rights, Civil Rights and Fair Housing Acts were signed.

After those Acts were signed, it appeared to many that the Movement achieved what it set out to achieve. That is to say, the Movement made America recognize the concept that Black Americans should be treated as equal citizens.

This recognition was only acknowledged on paper, not in practice. Sure, a few Black Americans were provided with a small number of opportunities. And when those few Black Americans were provided with those opportunities, it was as though the consensus thought in America was that each and every Black person was provided with those opportunities because a select few were.

On the Dick Cavett Show in 1968, James Baldwin was asked, "Why aren't the Negros optimistic? It's getting so much better; there are Negro mayors, there's Negros in all of sports, there are Negros in politics, they're even … in television commercials now. Is it at once getting much better and still hopeless?"

To which Baldwin explained with eerie foresight, "Well, I don't think there's much hope for it, you know … to tell you the truth. As long as people are using this peculiar language. It's not a question of what happens to the Negro here … to the Black man here. That's a very vivid question for me, you know. But the real question is what's going to happen to this country. I have to repeat that."

The question posed to Baldwin highlights the thinking then and now: so what that there may be systemic oppression against Black people in general, there are some Black people who have "made it" so all Black people should feel equal with white people and be successful like these few who have managed to be successful.

Since 1970, police, prosecutors and judges have continued to employ discriminating practices against Black Americans the same as they did during the Dred Scott days, the Homer Plessy days and during the Civil Rights era. The goal of America has been, and is, to maintain the thinking and practices that were used by the United States Supreme Court in the Dred Scott and Plessy v. Ferguson decisions (and numerous other decisions), the Jim Crow period, and during the previous Civil Rights era: keep Black Americans inferior to whites by engaging in physical and psychological warfare against them.

They are no longer saying outright, "separate, but equal," but they are practicing it. They are acting confused as to why more Black people are committing crimes while ignoring the obvious systematic attack on Black people by police, prosecutors and judges.

The studies unequivocally show that police are specifically targeting Black Americans, while at the same time being lenient with white Americans even though the same studies show that whites are more likely to possess contraband. Those studies, and there are multiple of them, answer the question, "Why do Black people commit more crimes?" The evidence-based answer is that police, prosecutors and judges make sure they do.

The evidence also reveals that once the police hand over Black Americans to the court system, prosecutors[18] (95% of whom are

---

[18] A 2015 study by the Women Donors Network found that in three-fifths of the states where prosecutors are elected, there isn't a single black prosecutor. Overall, the study found that in the United States, 95 percent of elected prosecutors are white, and

white in America) and judges continue the disproportionately harsh treatment. If you are a Black American you are almost for certain going to be charged with more serious crimes by the prosecutor (overcharging) and the judge will undoubtedly order that you serve a longer prison sentence than a white American.

In other words, when you stand before that judge you are in the same shoes that Dred Scott wore when the Court reasoned that his life as a Black man did not matter, that the rights in the U.S. Constitution did not apply to him and told him that he belonged to a group that was **"so far inferior, that they had no rights which the white man was bound to respect."**

The United States of America has, for the most part, still refused to respect the rights of Black Americans.

---

nearly 80 percent are white men. In nine death penalty states (Colorado, Delaware, Idaho, Montana, Oregon, South Dakota, Tennessee, Washington and Wyoming), all of the elected district attorneys were white in 2015.

The facts from those studies examining policing, prosecuting and judging Black Americans lead to no other conclusion than Dred Scott has yet to be overturned, in practice. The Equal Protection Clause of the 14th Amendment still does not apply to Black Americans. The 13th Amendment still has not provided the freedom it purportedly decrees. As such, the Civil Rights Movement continues and, with respect to addressing the racist Criminal Justice Regime, the responsibility for the Movement's success is now on you and your interaction with the police, prosecutors and judges.

The Criminal Justice Regime

This book focuses on your rights with respect to engaging with the police and the court system. The way that system attacks Black Americans, it is evident that the system is being used to continue the "white backlash" that has been occurring since Governor George Wallace swore that Jim Crow would live on. It is simply a regime that has been instilled in America to continue to circumvent the 13th Amendment and allow others to profit off of Black bodies. The prison system in the United States generates approximately $74 billion dollars per year.[19]

It is, therefore, critical that you learn the rights you have under the laws so that you can do your part in protecting yourself and fighting back against the Criminal Justice Regime. You are now accountable for learning and responsible for practicing those rights, because as Dr. Martin Luther King, Jr. wrote from a jail cell in Birmingham: "We know through painful experience that freedom is never voluntarily given by the oppressor; it must be demanded by the oppressed." You are a fool to continue to ask the Regime to respect your rights and to stop viewing you as inferior. Learn and practice your rights, respectfully.

---

[19] Brian Kincade, *The Economics of the American Prison System,* Smart Asset, https://smartasset.com/mortgage/the-economics-of-the-american-prison-system (last visited Dec. 1, 2018).

YOUR RIGHTS AND HOW TO USE THEM

There are three levels of the Criminal Justice Regime that your words flow through and will be used against you. The first level is the police; the second level is the prosecutor; and the third level is the judge.

If you choose to speak to the police officer who interrogates you, then what you are actually doing is giving the prosecutor ammunition to use against you in court. As soon as you are done speaking with the police officer (or, more accurately, as soon as the police officer has pulled every last word out of you that you will provide) that police officer goes straight to the prosecutor and tells them what evidence you have just provided against yourself. The prosecutor then decides if you have provided enough evidence against yourself, along with any other evidence they have against you, to charge you with a crime.

After the prosecutor uses your words to charge you with a crime, then the same prosecutor, during your court proceedings, tells the judge what you said and tries mightily to convince the judge to put you in prison.

There are two main reasons the police want to talk to you: 1) they have solid evidence against you but want you to put a bow on the evidence with a confession, or 2) the evidence they have against you is weak and they need your confession to fill in the cracks of that evidence. The police and prosecutors know that if they go to court with weak evidence, your lawyer will be able to attack and exploit those cracks and properly defend you.

While it may seem obvious to advise people not to speak to the police, approximately 90% of people waive their Miranda rights and choose to speak with police officers. As you will learn, there are specific techniques that the police use to get you to confess. Their intent, even from the moment they walk up to you on the street or stop you in a vehicle, is to throw you into the Criminal Justice Regime.

There are Rules of Engagement that govern battles. This book contains the Rules for you to employ during police interactions so you can avoid being consumed by the Regime.

Terry Stop

In the United States Supreme Court case of Terry v. Ohio,[20] the Court ruled that police officers can stop a person without a warrant in public and conduct a pat down search without violating the 4th Amendment's protections against unreasonable searches and seizures if the officer has **reasonable suspicion** to believe that the person is armed or involved in a crime.

Know the Law:

- A stop under Terry v. Ohio is known as a "Terry stop." A Terry stop is a **brief detention** of a person in order to conduct an investigatory search.

- The officer must be able to articulate the **specific facts** they are relying on to stop and frisk you.

---

[20] *Terry v. Ohio, 392 U.S. 1 (1968)*

- Overzealous officers will sometimes fabricate a story to get the reasonable suspicion needed to stop you. Ask that they turn their body camera on and then tell you the facts they are relying on to stop you. Get details, but do not engage in a conversation or argument with the officer. Just make them articulate the reasonable suspicion they are relying on for the stop.

- This stop is an involuntary stop because you are not free to leave and are required to remain with the officer until the officer has completed the investigatory search. Therefore, you are detained.

- The detention is required to be brief. The officer is only supposed to detain you for as long as it is necessary to obtain your name (if, 1) you are in a state that requires you to identify yourself, or 2) the baseline facts relied upon for the stop make knowing your name necessary to conduct the investigation) and conduct a search for weapons or contraband.

- Not every stop justifies a frisk. If you are frisked (also known as a pat down search), the police can only pat down your outer clothing (they can't reach under your clothes or into your pockets on the initial pat down), they cannot manipulate objects in your pockets to try to determine what the objects are (they are supposed to keep a flat hand while patting you down), and they can't take or search your cell phone.

- If a police officer feels what is known to be contraband or a weapon (without manipulating it in any way), then they can remove that item from your pocket or person and use it as evidence for an arrest.

- If you are being frisked, ask to have the officer's body camera turned on and narrate the search as it is happening. For example, if the officer squeezes an object in your pocket in order to determine what the object is, make sure to say that so that your attorney can use that information.

- Remember, the officer is not permitted to manipulate the object with their fingers in order to figure out what the object is.

- While you are narrating the search (saying what the officer is doing so that you have a recording of it and are not just going to rely on the police officer's report), make sure not to say anything other than the narration of the search. Do not make any statements that can be used against you in court.

- If the police conduct an illegal Terry stop and get evidence against you, your attorney can file a motion to suppress that evidence.

- A motion to suppress evidence is a motion based on the 4th Amendment protection against unreasonable searches and seizures. While the police are permitted to stop and frisk you if they have a proper basis to do so, if they violate any of the rules noted above, then what was originally a constitutional stop turns into an unconstitutional stop. If the judge grants your motion to suppress, then any evidence gained from the unconstitutional stop cannot be used against you in court.

- If you are successful with the motion to suppress, then your attorney can file a motion to dismiss the charges against you if the remaining evidence the police have against you is insufficient to support the charges in the indictment.

Examples of Reasonable Suspicion:

- Furtive (you will see police use this word often – it means you are trying to avoid being noticed or that you look guilty) action concealing suspected weapons or contraband.

- Standing lookout for others preparing to commit a suspected crime.

- Casing a retail shop or other potential crime location.

- The suspect's flight or evasive action attempting to elude police.

- Commission of crime nearby from which the suspect may have fled.

- Other witness's descriptions matching the suspect. This is the, "You match the description," pretext.

- Erratic behavior suggesting the suspect is under the influence. (This may not justify a search for weapons).

- Exchange of money suggesting a drug crime or solicitation to prostitution.

- Exchange of items that may be drugs or other contraband.

Cases Involving Terry Stops

- Because Terry Stops are common and lead to the most interaction and confrontation with police officers, here are examples of Terry stops and the outcome of the legality of the stop.

Illinois v. Caballes, 125 S.Ct. 834 (2005)

The defendant was stopped for a routine speeding violation. While the car was stopped and the trooper was preparing a warning ticket, another officer walked a drug dog around the car. The dog alerted; the car was searched based on probable cause; and drugs were found. The Supreme Court held that this was permissible. A dog alert is not a "search" and in this case, the time it took to walk the dog around the car did not prolong the stop. Thus, there was no Terry violation and no need for a warrant or an articulable suspicion to authorize the use of the dog.

Hiibel v. Sixth Judicial Dist. Court of Nev., 124 S.Ct. 2451 (2004)

The Supreme Court held that the police may require a person to identify himself if he is the subject of a lawful Terry stop; and if he fails to do so, he may be charged and convicted of a "refusal to identify" state offense. In this case, the police suspected that the defendant had been involved in a fight and they approached him and asked him to identify himself. He refused. The Court emphasized that requiring the suspect to identify himself was reasonably related to the basis for the initial detention and thus was a permissible extension of the Terry stop.

Maryland v. Wilson, 519 U.S. 408 (1997)

The police may direct a passenger to exit a vehicle where the car has been stopped for a legitimate reason.

Ohio v. Robinette, 519 U.S. 33 (1996)

If a lawful traffic stop has been made and the basis for the traffic stop has been accomplished, the police may then request consent to search the vehicle without announcing to the driver that he is free to leave. This is why it is important to clarify with the officer exactly when you are free to leave. This is likely when they have written the citation and provided you with a copy.

Arizona v. Johnson, 555 U.S. 323 (2009)

If the police stop a vehicle lawfully and there is a passenger in the vehicle, if the police have a reason to believe the passenger is armed and dangerous, he may be frisked. This is true even if the passenger is not believed to have committed any crime. This is justified based on officer safety.

United States v. Dapolito, 713 F.3d 141 (1st Cir. 2013)

At approximately 2:00 a.m., the police saw the defendant standing in the alcove of a building in downtown Portland, Maine. When questioned, he gave rambling, sometimes incoherent answers to questions. When the police called dispatch to determine whether there were any warrants, the response was negative. There was insufficient information to believe that he was engaged in any criminal activity or that he was wanted in any jurisdiction. The encounter, which lasted twenty minutes, and ultimately involved several officers, rose to the level of a detention when he was repeatedly asked to produce identification and to consent to a search, which he refused. The resulting frisk was the product of this illegal detention.

United States v. Davis, 430 F.3d 345 (6th Cir. 2005)

When a drug dog failed to alert to the defendant's car, which had been stopped on the highway, the police summoned a second drug dog. This unlawfully prolonged the duration of the stop (initially prompted by a speeding charge).

United States v. Washington, 387 F.3d 1060 (9th Cir. 2004)

The police went to the defendant's residential hotel room and knocked, with the expectation of gaining the defendant's consent to search the premises. But the defendant stepped outside the door when the police knocked and closed the door behind him. The police (six of them) repeatedly asked for permission to go in the apartment and reminded the defendant that he could be arrested on an unrelated matter. Eventually, the officers made their way inside and ultimately convinced the defendant to consent to a search. The Ninth Circuit found these Fourth Amendment violations: First the officers exceeded a Terry stop in the hallway; then they violated the defendant's rights by not allowing the door to remain closed; then they violated his rights by entering the apartment without his consent; and finally, they violated his rights by moving his jacket to find a small amount of methamphetamine. His subsequent consent to search was tainted by all of these previous violations.

Miranda Rights

In the United States Supreme Court case of Miranda v. Arizona,[21] the Court ruled that "the prosecution may not use statements, whether exculpatory or inculpatory, stemming from custodial interrogation of the defendant unless it demonstrates the use of procedural safeguards effective to secure the privilege against self-incrimination."

Know the Law:

- The Miranda warnings that you've heard on television and in movies came from the Miranda decision. Those warnings are, "You have the right to remain silent; Anything you say can and will be used against you in a court of law; You have the right to talk to a lawyer and have them present with you while you are being questioned; If you cannot afford to hire a lawyer, one will be appointed to represent you before any questioning, if you wish;

---

[21] *Miranda v. Arizona, 384 U.S. 436 (1966)*

You can decide at any time to exercise these rights and not answer any questions or make any statements."

- When police give a suspect these warnings, it is known as being "Mirandized."

- Your Miranda rights are rooted in the Fifth Amendment of the United States Constitution. The Fifth Amendment, among other rights, protects you against being a witness against yourself (self-incrimination).

- There are two main factors for your Miranda rights to be invoked: 1) you have to be in custody; and 2) police have to be interrogating you.

- In custody means that you are "deprived of your freedom in any way." In other words, you are not free to leave. **It is imperative that you ask the police if you are free to leave when having any interaction with them.** That question defines whether or not you are in custody, legally.

- The Miranda Court defined interrogation as, "questioning initiated by law enforcement officers after a person has been taken into custody or otherwise deprived of his freedom of action in any significant way."

- Interrogation includes express questioning (asking you questions directly), or its "functional equivalent."

- The U.S. Supreme Court in Rhode Island v. Innis[22] explained that the "term 'interrogation' under Miranda refers not only to express questioning, but also to any words or actions on the part of the police (other than those normally attendant to arrest and custody) that the police should know are reasonably likely to elicit an incriminating response from

---

[22] *Rhode Island v. Innis, 100 S.Ct. 1682 (1980)*

the suspect."

- You have Miranda rights because police used to use physical abuse to beat confessions out of people. There were a series of cases involving physical abuse where the confessions were deemed involuntary. Police then shifted to using psychological tactics against suspects.

- The Miranda Court highlighted: "we stress that the modern practice of in-custody interrogation is psychologically rather than physically oriented."

- Your Miranda rights are designed to protect you against those psychological tactics.

- A **major flaw in the Miranda warnings** is that they explain that you have the right to remain silent. But what the Miranda warnings don't tell you is that if you only remain silent, then that **silence can and will be used against you**.

- In order for you to have the right to remain silent, you cannot be silent: You have to verbally state that you are invoking your 5th Amendment right to silence **immediately upon arrest**.

- After you are arrested (in custody) but before you are provided with your Miranda rights (before you are Mirandized), if you remain silent, then your silence can be used against you in court.

- In addition, if you are not in custody but the police are interrogating you, then your silence will be used against you. In Salinas v. Texas,[23] the United States Supreme Court held that when a defendant goes to the police station voluntarily and the police question him (in this case for an hour or so) and he answers some questions but not others, the prosecutor is free to use the fact that the person was

---

[23] *Salinas v. Texas, 133 S. Ct. 2174 (2013)*

silent against them.

- This will occur when a police officer just asks if you want to answer a few questions, or if you want to meet them at the station so you can talk about the case. Because you are meeting with the police at your own free will, you are not really in custody. That's why it is important to ask if you are free to leave. And never voluntarily go to the police station or speak with a police officer without an attorney present. When you are talking to the police, you are essentially speaking to the prosecutor. And the only reason the police want to talk to you is to gather evidence against you.

- In the Salinas case, the police were investigating a double murder and the investigation led to Salinas. Salinas agreed to go to the police station (so he was not in custody) to talk with the police. He talked with them for about an hour and when he was asked about the shell casing found at the scene he didn't say anything.

That silence was used against him at trial and the U.S. Supreme Court said it was legal to do so.

Interrogation Tactics

Know the Law:

- If you have failed to exercise your rights and choose to speak with the police, then you will be questioned by police officers that are trained to get you to confess.

- Approximately 90% of suspects waive their Miranda rights and choose to answer questions during a custodial interrogation.

- The problem is that people think they can tell a story to get out of the potential charges they were arrested for. You are not simply talking with a police officer when you are in an interrogation room. You are talking with a police officer who is highly trained in specific techniques that are utilized against you in order for you to confess.

- Remember, the Miranda Court specifically observed in their decision that the police switched from physically beating confessions out of suspects to psychologically beating confessions out of suspects.

- The specific interrogation technique that the police officers utilize against you is called the Reid Technique.

- The Reid Technique can be found in the book written by Fred E. Inbau, et al., titled, Criminal Interrogation and Confessions (5th ed. 2013). This book was first published in 1962 when the courts began throwing out confessions based on physical abuse. The book was revised after the Miranda decision. The Miranda Court referenced the book in their decision.

- The Reid Technique utilizes a 9-step process that is designed to manipulate your mind so that you end up confessing.

- What interrogators will do initially is leave you in the interrogation room for an extended period, maybe an hour or so, by yourself. This solitary confinement raises your level of anxiety and stress. You are likely being recorded during this time so it is advisable not to say anything. Police have obtained incriminating evidence from suspects when suspects begin talking to themselves in interrogation rooms when left alone for extended periods of time.

- Once an officer enters the interrogation room, they will begin to employ the Reid Technique (although some experts feel the isolation step is the first step of the Reid Technique), starting with step one: early confrontation. The officer will tell the suspect that the evidence appears to be indicating that they committed the crime. If the evidence is strong, the officer will be more forceful with this allegation.

- The second step is to develop a theme as to why the crime occurred. This theme will include a scenario that shifts the blame away from the suspect, or they develop themes containing reasons that will psychologically justify or excuse the crime. The police will develop or change the themes until they find one that you are responsive to.

- Step three, which is denials by the suspect, goes hand-in-hand with step four, which is objections made by the suspect. First, the suspect will deny facts that are part of the theme. Police are taught to ignore those denials, or keep the denials to a minimum. An innocent person will put up the strongest fight at the denial stage. Then, the suspect will object with something like, "I wouldn't commit that crime because I have too much to lose." Police officers are taught to accept these objections as truth and not to pick them apart, but also to use the objection to further develop the theme.

- In step five, police are trained to refocus your attention on them and the theme they are creating and not the punishment that may come from the crime. Police do this by getting physically closer to you and making eye contact.

- Step six is where the police officer will reintroduce the psychological justification for committing the crime and act sympathetic towards the suspect. Officers may say something like, "I can understand why you would want to get money for your family."

- Step seven can be said to be the most critical step in the interrogation process. This is where the interrogator will offer an alternate question to the suspect with both answers establishing guilt. For example, "Were you in the back seat or the passenger seat?" If you answer that question, then you put yourself in the vehicle. Or, "Was this robbery planned out, or did it just sorta happen spur of the moment?" Police are instructed to infer that the answer is probably the more morally acceptable answer.

- If you answer the question in step seven, then step eight is when the police officer will immediately say something to reinforce your statement and acknowledge what you said. Then they will ask you to say what happened in basic or general terms. They will also develop corroborating information to establish the validity of the confession.

- The final step is having you provide an official statement/confession, either in written or oral form. Just prior to having you provide the statement, they will likely give you Miranda warnings again. But by this time, you have already confessed.

- So, again, you are not simply having a conversation with a police officer when you are in an interrogation room. They are utilizing a decades-old technique that has been specifically designed to break you down mentally and get you to talk and confess. That's probably why 90% of suspects don't invoke their Miranda rights and choose to talk.

* In the United States Supreme Court case of Frazier v. Cupp,[24] the Supreme Court determined that police are permitted to use deceptive tactics during interrogation. In other words, along with the psychological tactics they can use against you, police officers are also allowed to lie to you during an interrogation. They can tell you that they have evidence that they don't really have, such as your fingerprints at the crime scene; they can tell you they have a witness who identified you; they can lie about the potential prison sentence you are facing; and they can tell you that your friend in the next interrogation room is talking and the one who talks first gets the best plea deal, or they can say they have your DNA evidence at the crime

---

[24] *Frazier v. Cupp,* 394 *U.S.* 731 (1969)

scene, among many other lies they can come up with. By the way, police officers have no power to give you a plea deal or to help you get a better plea deal if you "help them out." That's a function of the prosecutor's office.

- There are only three states that prohibit police from lying **to minors** during custodial interrogations (Illinois, Oregon and New York). This only applies to minors.

Pretextual Traffic Stops

Know the Law:

- Almost every day in the United States, police officers pull over approximately 50,000 drivers – more than 20 million people per year.

- A pretextual vehicle stop is when the police pull a motorist over for a minor infraction but their true motivation is to search the vehicle or passengers.

- In the United States Supreme Court case of Whren v. United States,[25] the Court found that pretextual stops were constitutional regardless of the true motivation of the police officer, which could likely be racial profiling.

- But, police are only allowed to detain you for as long as it takes to issue the citation and cannot keep you detained any longer than necessary. Sometimes the police will call for a K-9 unit to conduct a search while they are writing the citation. This is legal so long as it does not prolong the stop.

- The Oregon Supreme Court ruled that police could no longer pull someone over for a broken taillight or failure to signal,

---

[25] *Whren v. United States, 517 U.S. 806 (1996)*

then ask unrelated questions, such as asking for consent to search the car for illegal drugs or guns.

- Some things that could form the basis for a pretextual stop are a broken license plate light, anything hanging from your rearview mirror, tinted windows, failure to signal, among many other infractions.

- The fact of the matter is that if a police officer wants to pull you over, they can come up with a reason to do so. There are a plethora of vehicle codes and you are surely going to violate one while driving, especially if a police officer is following you and you are nervous.

- Stanford University and New York University analyzed a dataset of nearly 100 million traffic stops across the country over nearly a decade. White drivers, they found, were searched 1.5 to 2 times less often than Black drivers, but were more likely to have drugs, guns or other contraband. Black drivers were less likely to be stopped after sunset, when a 'veil of darkness' masks one's race, suggesting bias in stop decisions.

- Try to limit the reasons a police officer can pull your vehicle over. And if you are pulled over, then ask for the reason and then ask for the citation. It is important to establish the exact moment you are free to leave because that moment determines if the officer is prolonging the stop unconstitutionally.

Vehicle Searches

Know the Law:

- The Fourth Amendment to the U.S. Constitution limits the police's ability to search your vehicle.

- Once you have been pulled over by a police officer, the officer can search your vehicle if you give consent for them to conduct the search. I can't think of any reason to give an officer consent to search your vehicle.

- The officer can search your vehicle if they have a warrant to do so. This is not the typical situation but if they do have a warrant to search your vehicle you are allowed to see it first. Make sure the warrant is actually signed by a judge, and look to see if the warrant limits the areas to be searched, such as only the trunk or glove box.

- The officer can also search your vehicle if the officer has probable cause to believe that you have incriminating evidence inside your vehicle. For example, the police can search your car if your eyes are bloodshot and marijuana use is suspected, or if your car matches the description of a getaway vehicle used in a bank robbery. This search can include a locked glove box and the trunk, according to California

v. Acevedo[26]: "The police may search an automobile and the containers within it where they have probable cause to believe contraband or evidence is contained."

- The officer can also search the vehicle if the officer believes that a search is necessary for their own protection. This search should be limited to the driver's immediate area, which would include the glove box.

- If you have been arrested, then the police can search your vehicle. This will be called an inventory search where the police will say they need to inventory everything in your vehicle prior to towing it.

- In Pennsylvania v. Mimms,[27] the United States Supreme Court held that "once a motor vehicle has been lawfully detained for a traffic violation, the police officers may order the driver to get out of the

[26] *California v. Acevedo, 500 U.S. 565 (1991)*

[27] *Pennsylvania v. Mimms, 434 U. S. 106 (1977)*

vehicle without violating the Fourth Amendment," because the government's "legitimate and weighty" interest in officer safety outweighs the minor additional intrusion of requiring a driver, already lawfully stopped, to exit the vehicle. The officer may then pat down the driver under Terry v. Ohio.

- In Arizona v. Johnson,[28] the U.S. Supreme Court also decided that if a passenger is in the vehicle, then the police officer can make the passenger get out of the vehicle and be searched if the officer believes that the passenger is armed and dangerous or presents a threat to the officer.

- If an officer stops you for a minor violation and there is no evidence of any other crime, then they generally cannot search your vehicle (because they don't have probable cause) unless there is a basis for them to think you are a threat to them. Make them identify what the facts

---

[28] *Arizona v. Johnson, 555 U.S. 323 (2009)*

are that justify the search.

- If an officer sees evidence of contraband in plain view inside your vehicle, then they are permitted to search your vehicle with respect to the object that they saw. The same applies if they smell marijuana for people who live in states where marijuana is not legal. Under the plain view search exception, the police officer cannot simply search your vehicle generally – the search must be related to the item they saw or smelled.

- If a K-9 Unit drug sniffing dog is called to the scene where you are pulled over, the U.S. Supreme Court in Illinois v. Caballes[29] determined that allowing the dog to sniff for drugs around the outside of your vehicle is not considered a search and the police are permitted to do so without a warrant.

---

[29] *Illinois v. Caballes, 125 S.Ct. 834 (2005)*

- The Supreme Court reasoned that a dog alert is not a "search" and the time it takes to walk a dog around a vehicle does not prolong a stop. Thus, there is no Terry violation and no need for a warrant or an articulable suspicion to authorize the use of the dog. This exception only applies if calling the K-9 unit to the scene does not prolong the vehicle stop. If getting the dog to the scene prolongs the stop, then the police officers are not permitted to use the dog to sniff the vehicle.

- The Supreme Court has also decided[30] that once a traffic stop is concluded, then any search thereafter is considered to have exceeded the time reasonably required to handle the stop and that any search would violate the 4th Amendment's protections against unreasonable searches and seizures.

---

[30] *Rodriguez v. United States, 575 U.S. 348 (2015)*

Search Incident to Arrest

Know the Law:

- In Chimel v. California,[31] the United States Supreme Court explained, "when an arrest is made, it is reasonable for the arresting officer to search the person arrested in order to remove any weapons that the latter might seek to use in order to resist arrest or effect his escape. Otherwise, the officer's safety might well be endangered, and the arrest itself frustrated. In addition, it is entirely reasonable for the arresting officer to search for and seize any evidence on the arrestee's person in order to prevent its concealment or destruction. And the area into which an arrestee might reach in order to grab a weapon or evidentiary items must, of course, be governed by a like rule. A gun on a table or in a drawer in front of someone who is arrested can be as dangerous to the arresting officer as

---

[31] *Chimel v. California, 395 U.S. 752 (1969)*

one concealed in the clothing of the person arrested. There is ample justification, therefore, for a search of the arrestee's person and the area 'within his immediate control'—construing that phrase to mean the area from within which he might gain possession of a weapon or destructible evidence."

- This means that once you are arrested, the police are permitted to conduct a warrantless search of you and the immediate area around you. This search could be the area in your vehicle. But the U.S. Supreme Court clarified in Arizona v. Gant,[32] that the police can only search your vehicle after you are arrested if you are within reaching distance of the passenger compartment at the time of the search or it is reasonable to believe that the vehicle contains evidence of the offense of arrest.

---

[32] *Arizona v. Gant, 556 U.S. 332 (2009)*

- If the search incident to arrest occurs in your residence, then the police are not permitted to search every room in the home, or every drawer in the desk; the police would need a search warrant to search anything that is beyond your immediate area while being arrested.

- But if there are other people in the residence, then police may conduct a "protective sweep" of the home if officers have a reasonable suspicion that a person in the residence poses a threat.

Police Knock on Your Door

Know the Law:

- If the police show up to your home, it is advisable not to let them in your home. You should ask, through the door with the door closed, if they have a warrant.

- If the police do not have a warrant to enter or search your home, then you do not have to open the door for them.

- If the officers don't have a warrant then make it clear that you do not want to speak with them.

- In Mapp v. Ohio,[33] the United States Supreme Court ruled that if police illegally search you or your home, then the evidence they obtain during the illegal search cannot be used against you in court. In Mapp, police searched a woman's home without a warrant (even though they said they had a warrant and showed her a piece of paper) and found "obscene" materials. Police said they wanted to search her home to look for a suspect in a local bombing but the woman refused the let the police in her home. The police eventually forced their way in the home and found the "obscene" materials. The Supreme Court created the

---

33 *Mapp v. Ohio, 367 U.S. 643 (1961)*

exclusionary rule in Mapp by finding that illegally obtained evidence cannot be used in state court (that was already the rule in federal court).

- If police do have a warrant to search your home, then ask to see it through the peephole or they can slip it under the door or hold it against a window so you can read it.

- When you read the warrant, make sure that a judge signed it. Also, make note of the areas the warrant allows the officers to search (which rooms and for what items).

- If the warrant has a defect, then tell the officers what that defect is and that you are not consenting to the search. If they insist on searching based on the warrant, then make sure to video yourself and the fact that you are not consenting to the search.

- You can ask to watch the search. If permitted, then take video evidence of what the officers are searching.

- Here is a case that shows the best way to handle the police attempting to search your home:

United States v. Washington, 387 F.3d 1060 (9th Cir. 2004)

The police went to the defendant's residential hotel room and knocked, with the expectation of gaining the defendant's consent to search the premises. But the defendant stepped outside the door when the police knocked and closed the door behind him. The police (six of them) repeatedly asked for permission to go in the apartment and reminded the defendant that he could be arrested on an unrelated matter. Eventually, the officers made their way inside and ultimately convinced the defendant to consent to a search. The Ninth Circuit found these Fourth Amendment violations: First the officers exceeded a Terry stop in the hallway; then they violated the defendant's rights by not allowing the door to remain closed; then they violated his rights by entering the apartment without his consent; and finally, they violated his rights by moving his jacket to find a small amount of methamphetamine. His subsequent consent to search was tainted (invalid and unenforceable) by all of these previous violations.

Border Stops

Know the Law:

- The United States Supreme Court has made clear that an individual's rights to privacy and 4th Amendment protection against unreasonable searches and seizures are limited at international borders. This includes areas up to 100 miles from the border and federal officers, such as the Border Patrol, conduct the searches and seizures.

- The rules regulating searches and seizures at the actual border or ports of entry are different than the rules regulating searches and seizures away from the border that are done by federal officers.

- The U.S. Supreme Court has made a distinction between searches of people versus vehicles. Vehicles receive less 4th Amendment protection than people.

- For searches of a person at a border or port of entry, federal officers may conduct routine inspections and searches of persons attempting to cross the international border without a warrant or any particularized suspicion of unlawful activity.

- But a border search that extends beyond a routine search and inspection may require at least reasonable suspicion.

- While the Supreme Court has not specifically told us what qualifies as a routine border search of a person, the Court has implied that highly intrusive searches, such as body cavity searches, may fall outside the reasonable suspicion requirement and necessitate a higher level of suspicion to comply with the 4th Amendment.

- In United States v. Montoya de Hernandez,[34] the U.S. Supreme Court found that overnight detention for monitored bowel movement followed by rectal examination is "beyond the scope of a routine customs search" and permissible under the border exception only with reasonable suspicion.

- With respect to vehicles at the border, however, the Supreme Court ruled in United States v. Flores-Montano[35] that federal officers had the authority to disassemble and inspect a vehicle's fuel tank without any suspicion (it qualified as a routine search).

---

[34] *United States v. Montoya de Hernandez, 473 U.S. 531 (1985)*

[35] *United States v. Flores-Montano, 541 U.S. 149 (2004)*

- Agents are not permitted to engage in "roving patrols" where they stop vehicles at random on highways. In order to stop a vehicle driving on a highway, the federal agent must have reasonable suspicion of an immigration violation or crime, but probable cause is required to search the vehicle for contraband or other evidence of a crime.

- The Border Patrol is permitted to have fixed checkpoints where they stop each vehicle that comes through the checkpoint.

- At the checkpoint, agents are permitted to ask occupants of the vehicle about their citizenship and to visually examine the outside of the vehicle.

- Agents are also permitted to have you pull outside of the normal checkpoint and into a secondary inspection area where they can ask you additional questions limited to your citizenship.

- The detention at the secondary inspection location should be brief and should not consist of prolonged questioning.

- You do have the right to remain silent regarding your citizenship, but if you do remain silent you can expect to have a much lengthier stay at the checkpoint area.

- Federal officers must have probable cause to search vehicles at the checkpoints.

DUI Stops

Know the Law:

- Some states permit DUI sobriety checkpoints to be set up on roadways in order to check for impaired drivers.

- Generally, the 4th Amendment of the United States Constitution would not permit such a search because there is no reasonable suspicion or probable cause at a sobriety checkpoint – the police are stopping and searching every vehicle that comes through the checkpoint. The United States Supreme Court in Michigan Dep't of State Police v. Sitz,[36] however, determined that the importance of keeping impaired drivers off the road generally outweighs the inconvenience and intrusion to motorists and allowed the temporary detention and search.

- If you make a U-turn to avoid a checkpoint then that can be a factor in the police making the decision to conduct a vehicle stop, and is a violation of the law in some states. Certainly, if you violate any traffic law in avoiding a checkpoint then police can pull you over.

- In some states (check your local laws) you are permitted to not roll down your window at the checkpoint but must provide all necessary documentation to

---

[36] *Michigan Dep't of State Police v. Sitz, 496 U.S. 444 (1990)*

the officer. Drivers have placed their driver's license, registration and proof of insurance in a plastic bag and hung it outside the window so the officers can access the documents. This may not work in your state.

• At DUI checkpoints, the officers will ask you if you have had any alcohol to drink. If you say no, then you should be permitted to leave. If you say yes, or if the officer observes signs of intoxication, then they can ask you to perform a breathalyzer test and possibly field sobriety tests.

• Miranda protections do not apply to DUI sobriety checkpoints. Police are not required to give you Miranda warnings prior to your interaction with them at the checkpoint.

• Once police make a DUI arrest, the implied consent laws of all states require the arrested driver to take a chemical test (typically, of the breath or blood) at the officer's request.

- If you refuse to provide the blood, then the police generally will get a warrant to obtain your blood.

- If you are stopped for suspicion of driving under the influence then, as with all interactions with the police, you should not make any statements. Generally, it is best if you do not participate in any field sobriety tests and any preliminary breath tests and submit to a chemical or blood test only if you are arrested. In other words, minimize any probable cause the officer may be looking for to effectuate an arrest.

- Some drivers have a dash cam so they can record their interactions with police and provide their own evidence (such as if a police officer says the driver has watery, bloodshot eyes, and the driver shows his eyes in the camera and they are not, in fact, watery or bloodshot).

QUICK REFERENCE GUIDE

Police Stop You In Public, aka "Terry Stop"

What Happens: A police officer stops you in public to ask you a few questions – the officer may say you match the description of someone they are looking for.

What You Should Do:

1. Tell the officer your name, if you are required to do so.[37]

2. Ask if you are free to leave.

3. If the officer says yes, then leave without saying anything.

---

[37] There are 26 states where you are obligated to identify yourself to a police officer during a Terry stop. Those states are listed at the end of this book.

4. If the officer says no, then ask the officer to articulate the reasonable suspicion they are relying on for the stop. Do not engage in a conversation or argument with the officer about what they say is the reasonable suspicion.

5. Next, inform the officer that you are invoking your 5th Amendment right to remain silent (you have to say that you are invoking your rights, otherwise your rights may not protect you) and that you would like a lawyer present during any questioning.

6. Call the local Public Defender's Office in your area so that an attorney can be present on your behalf.

7. Do not say another word.

Interrogation Room

What Happens: The police bring you to the police station for questioning or you come to the police station on your own.

What You Should Do:

1. Identify yourself as needed (only your name).

2. If you are placed in an interrogation room you should expect that the police will leave you in that room for an extended period of time in isolation. This is on purpose to raise your stress and anxiety levels.

3. It is highly likely that you are being recorded even if you are by yourself in the interrogation room so you should remain silent or speak loudly and say that you are invoking your 5th Amendment rights and want a lawyer present prior to any questioning.

4. Once someone does come into the interrogation room ask them if you are free to leave.

5. If the officer says that you are free to leave, then leave without saying anything.

6. If the officer says that you are not free to leave, then say that you are invoking your 5th Amendment right to remain silent (you have to say that you are invoking your rights, otherwise your rights may not protect you) and that you would like a lawyer present during any questioning.

8. Call the local Public Defender's Office in your area so that an attorney can be present on your behalf.

9. Do not say another word, no matter what. Remember, police can and do lie to suspects during questioning. It is important to have a lawyer present. If you do choose to answer questions,

the police will begin to utilize the Reid Technique explained above. You should have a lawyer present to protect your rights.

Vehicle Stop

What Happens: A police officer pulls your vehicle over or approaches your vehicle while you are sitting in the vehicle.

What You Should Do:

1. Remain calm.

2. Turn on a video – either a dash cam or your cell phone. It is preferable that you are not holding the cell phone but rather it is secured in a cellphone holder of some type.

3. Respectfully, ask the police officer why they pulled you over – this will set the ground rules to any searches.

4. Do not answer any of their questions and inform them that you are invoking your right to remain silent under the 5th Amendment.

5. They will attempt to talk to you like you are just having a friendly conversation with them – do not talk with them at all. Continue to invoke your 5th Amendment rights.

6. Provide them with your license, registration and proof of insurance.

7. Do not give any consent to search your vehicle – the 4th Amendment protects you from unreasonable searches and seizures.

8. If they have a warrant to search your vehicle, check the validity of the warrant and then let them search your vehicle. Make sure the warrant is signed and also check the areas of the vehicle the warrant allows them to search. The search of the vehicle

should be limited to just those areas listed on the warrant.

9. If they say there is probable cause to search your vehicle, then have the officer articulate what the probable cause is for the video you should be recording.

10. If they ask you to exit the vehicle, then tell them you will exit the vehicle but you would like to know the basis for their request (they will likely say it is for their safety or protection).

11. If they ask any passengers in the vehicle to get out of the vehicle, have them comply with the request.

12. Once you are outside of the vehicle, the police may conduct a pat down search of you, which is permitted.

13. Again, do not answer any questions – continue to invoke your 5th Amendment rights and ask to have a

lawyer present for any questioning.

14. Once you are back inside the vehicle, ask if you are free to leave. Try to determine the exact moment you are free to leave. Police are not permitted to prolong a detention. If they do, then the search and seizure becomes unconstitutional.

15. Never be hostile towards the police.

Police Knock on Your Door

What Happens: The police show up to your home and knock on your door.

What You Should Do:

1. Do not open the door or allow them to see inside of your home – use the peephole only. Under the "Plain View Doctrine," if the police see contraband or evidence of a crime inside your home, then they can search your home with respect to those items or seize them.

2. Speak to the officers through the door.

3. Tell them you are not consenting to any search of your home.

4. If they have a warrant, ask to read the warrant before they enter the home.

5. Have them put the warrant in a place where you can read the details of the warrant and see that a judge signed the warrant.

6. If the warrant is valid, then allow the officers to enter your home.

7. Remain calm during the interaction.

8. Ask to remain in the home and either take notes of what the officers are doing or video their search.

9. If you are not allowed to stay in the home while the search is being conducted (usually the police will say you cannot because of officer safety), then calmly leave and wait outside.

10. Do not answer any questions – inform the officers that you are invoking your 5th Amendment rights and would like an attorney present prior to any questioning.

11. The officers may attempt to engage in "friendly" conversation with you. Do not speak to the officers at all. Inform them that you are invoking your 5th Amendment rights and would like an attorney present during any questioning.

12. If they find evidence of a crime and ask you about it, do not say anything other than you are invoking your 5th Amendment rights and would like a lawyer present during any questioning. Make sure to respond in that way because if you say nothing, then your silence may end up being used against you.

STOP AND IDENTIFY STATES

As of the publication of this book, the following states require you to identify yourself during a Terry Stop.

Alabama	Ala. Code §15-5-30
Arizona	Ari. Rev. Stat. Tit. 13, §2412 (enacted 2005) & Tit. 28, §1595
Arkansas	Ark. Code Ann. [1]§ 5-71-213
Colorado	Colo. Rev. Stat. §16-3-103(1)
Delaware	Del. Code Ann., Tit. 11, §§1902 (requires suspicion of a crime), 1321(6)(in the context of loitering)
Florida	Fla. Stat. §901.151 (Stop and Frisk Law); §856.021(2) (loitering and prowling)
Georgia	Ga. Code Ann. §16-11-36(b)
Illinois	Ill. Comp. Stat., ch. 725, §5/107-14
Indiana	Indiana Code IC §34-28-5-3.5
Kansas	Kan. Stat. Ann. §22-2402(1)

Louisiana	La. Code Crim. Proc. Ann., Art. 215.1(A); La. Rev. Stat. 14:108(B)(1)(c)
Maryland	Md. Criminal Code §4-206
Missouri	Mo. Rev. Stat. §84.710(2) (Kansas City Only)
Montana	Mont. Code Ann. §46-5-401
Nebraska	Neb. Rev. Stat. §29-829
Nevada	Nev. Rev. Stat. §171.123
New Hampshire	N.H. Rev. Stat. Ann. §594:2, §644:6
New Mexico	N.M. Stat. Ann. §30-22-3
New York	N.Y. Crim. Proc. Law Laws of New York → CPL §140.50 (requires suspicion of crime)
North Carolina	State v Friend + N.C. Gen.Stat. § 14–223
North Dakota	N.D. Cent. Code §29-29-21 (PDF)
Ohio	Ohio Rev. Code §2921.29 (enacted 2006)
Rhode Island	R.I. Gen. Laws §12-7-1
Utah	Utah Code Ann. §77-7-15
Vermont	Vt. Stat. Ann., Tit. 24, §1983
Wisconsin	Wis. Stat. §968.24

Made in the USA
Columbia, SC
17 December 2021